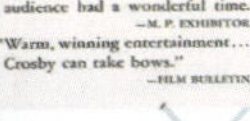

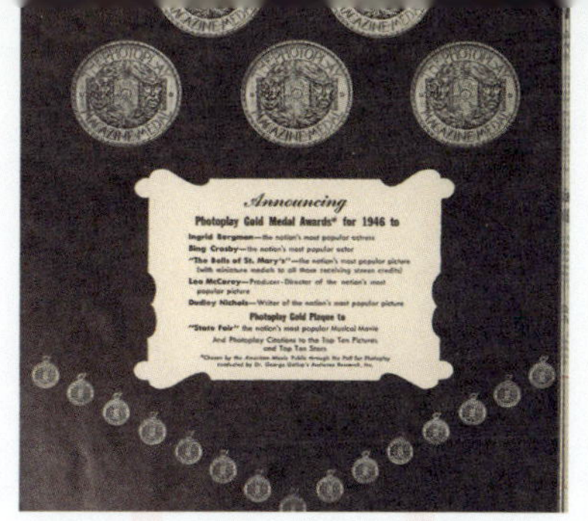

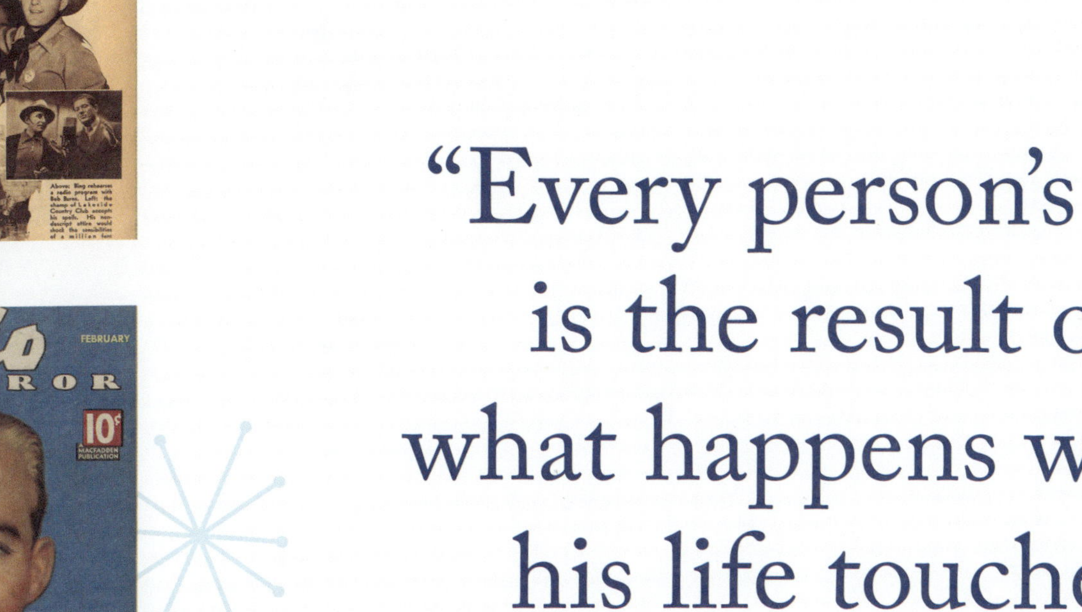
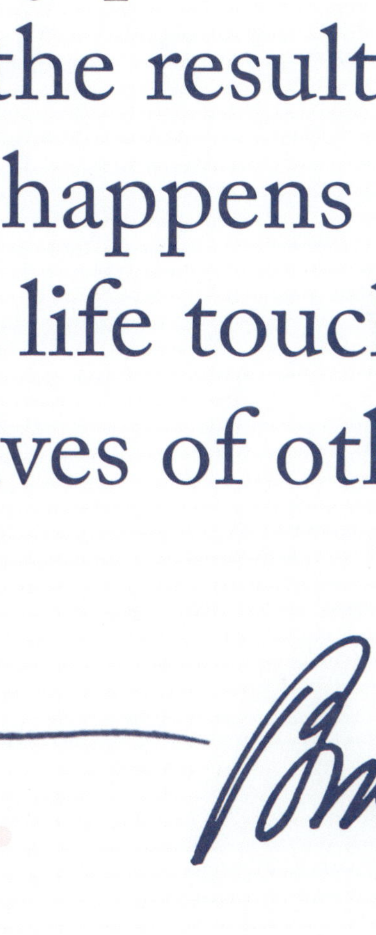

"Every person's life
is the result of
what happens when
his life touches
the lives of others."

— 

To Michael Waldrip, our multitalented brother and friend.
"Do you see a man skilled in his work?
He will stand before kings" (Proverbs 22:29).

—L. R. H.

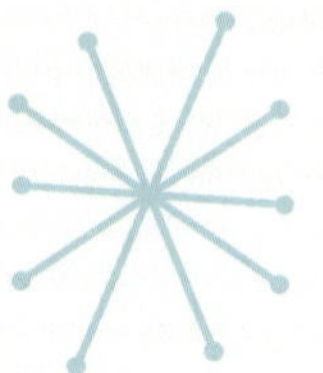

To Marilyn Garrison, my former art teacher.
You ignited a spark in me that created an art wildfire.
Thank you for teaching me the rules of art,
so that I could break them!

—J. D. E.

Text by Lauren R. Harris
Art by Joe Everson

First Edition, October 2025
10 9 8 7 6 5 4 3 2 1
Printed in China

This book is set in Lato and Adobe Caslon Pro.
Designed by MelindaMartin.me. Proofread by Beth Lottig, Inspire Books.
The paintings for this book were created with acrylic on canvas.

ISBN: 978-1-57102-794-8
Library of Congress Control Number: 2025943153

Photos provided by HLC Properties, LTD; Ron Bosley Collection, Bing Crosby Advocates; Bing Crosby Collection, Foley Center Library, Gonzaga University; Julian P. Graham Photo/Pebble Beach Company Lagorio Archives.

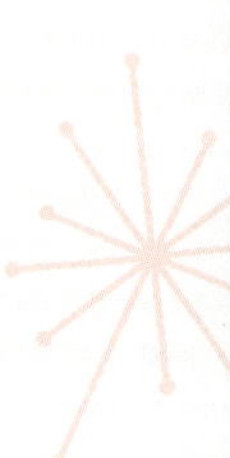

Gonzaga University Dramatic Club, 1920

BING HIMSELF

The Story of Bing Crosby, the World's First Multimedia Star

Lauren R. Harris

Art by Joe Everson

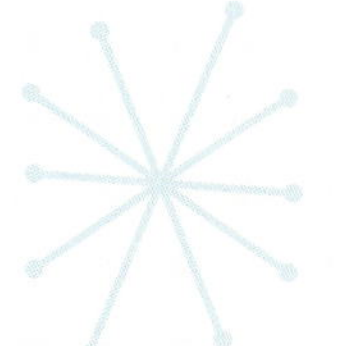

AMY LANE

Bing Crosby grew up in a cozy bungalow built by his father and uncles on the edge of Gonzaga University's campus in Spokane, Washington. Bing and his six siblings gathered around the fireplace while their father played Irish folk songs on the mandolin. Bing's father bought the family an Edison phonograph, one of the first record players in town. The family played song after song in their living room. Bing sang at the top of his voice.

"I guess I started singing
as soon as I started talking."

Bing's real name was Harry Lillis Crosby. Each week, he read a newspaper cartoon called *The Bingville Bugle*. He talked about these cartoons so much that his friends nicknamed him "Bingo," later shortened to "Bing." He and his friends roamed the neighborhood, playing baseball in spring, swimming in summer, picking apples in autumn, and sledding in winter.

"I have traveled many different 'Roads'
in my motion picture career,
but that road up Lidgerwood Hill
brings to my mind the sweetest memories of all."

Bing excelled at sports, especially baseball, and he hummed, whistled, or sang everywhere he went.

"I had a constant succession of songs in my head. And I had to whistle or sing to get them out."

Bing's mother arranged for him to sing at church gatherings, ladies' meetings, and community events. She dressed him in frilly ties and knee pants, which Bing didn't like. But he liked to sing, so he would perform anyway.

At school, Bing was best known by teachers and classmates for his clever pranks and witty jokes. He memorized poetry and literature in several languages and acted out Shakespeare plays in theater groups.

"We had a lot of experience in public speaking and debating, standing on your feet, talking, and doing plays, and if I have ability as an actor, that's where I got it."

Bing worked many jobs and saved enough money to buy a small drum and cymbal set. He quickly learned to play, and after high school, he joined a band called The Musicaladers, which became popular around Spokane. Originally hired to sweep floors at the local theater, Bing worked his way up to singing in between silent movies.

"When you're doing what you like to do, really, it isn't work, it's fun."

Bing studied to be a lawyer at Gonzaga University. During class, he drummed rhythms with his pencil and composed songs in his head. He often left early to play with the Musicaladers or sing at the theater. Bing's bandmate, Al Rinker, had a famous sister who sang with a band in Hollywood, California. Bing and Al decided they could become professional musicians, too. Before Bing's graduation, they bought an old car and drove from Spokane to Hollywood, singing wherever they could earn a few dollars.

"I told my parents I would rather sing than eat."

In Hollywood, Al's sister helped them get auditions to sing at a local theater. After several small concerts, the two friends joined an international traveling show. Bing studied the techniques of the seasoned performers in the show.

> "Although I wasn't a musician,
> and I'm still not one,
> I learned to appreciate
> good things when I heard them
> and to recognize bad things
> and avoid them."

The band played while vocalists sang into a new invention, the electric microphone. Most singers stood away from it, singing loudly. But Bing leaned in close, creating a soothing, conversational sound. He combined scat-style lyrics with expressive, improvised phrases. Bing didn't like rehearsing, and during recording sessions he chewed gum, read a newspaper, or held his pipe in his mouth. This casual approach gave Bing's voice a sincere quality appealing to all types of people.

A big record company offered him a contract, and a radio network hired him for weekly shows. Bing's crooning *boo-boo-boo-boo* filled millions of homes.

Bing was offered small roles in the new talking pictures. Movie directors thought his ears stuck out too far, and he was too short to be a leading man. However, audiences enjoyed Bing's cheerful, carefree characters who relied on charm and quick wit to succeed. Bing added puns and slang words that he used in real life, making his acting even more relatable.

"All I ever did was play myself."

Movie plots introduced new songs for Bing to sing, which became instant hits. Soon, Bing was the star of several movies a year. He admired his talented costars, so he decided that supporting actors in all his movies would get their names promoted equally alongside his. Bing acted, narrated, and sang in 104 films, including a Disney cartoon. His movies sold over a billion tickets, and 14 of his songs were nominated for Academy Awards. Bing won an Oscar for his 1944 film, *Going My Way*, a lighthearted musical drama.

"This is the only country in the world
where an old, broken-down crooner
can win an Oscar for acting.
It shows that everybody in this country
has a chance to succeed."

LOUIS BROW

Bing married a popular movie star, Dixie Lee, and they had four sons. He built a big house in Los Angeles for his family and another down the street for his parents. His father and brothers managed his performances and investments.

People all over the world heard Bing's voice on records, on the radio, or acting and singing in movies. Wherever Bing went, crowds pressed in to take photos with him and ask him for autographs.

"I love to sing, and I can thank my lucky stars that other people like to hear me!"

He anonymously gave away much of his money, helping people in need or building churches and orphanages. He offered jobs to out-of-work actors or crew members. Bing even made time in his busy schedule to promote local fundraisers in his hometown of Spokane.

During the Great Depression, people felt worried and discouraged. Bing's warm baritone lifted their spirits with songs like "Wrap Your Troubles in Dreams" and "Ac-Cent-Tchu-Ate the Positive." Several of his songs earned Gold Records. He popularized many styles of American music: jazz, Western, Hawaiian, folk ballads, and holiday favorites, including church hymns like "Silent Night."

"Anybody who wants to be a singer,
I think they should sing, sing, sing, every opportunity they get."

After the bombing of Pearl Harbor on December 7, 1941, Bing sang "White Christmas" for the first time on his weekly radio show, comforting fearful Americans with the song's sentimental message and connecting Bing's silvery voice with the holidays. To this day, Bing's "White Christmas" is the best-selling song of all time.

"It's a great song with a simple melody,
and nowadays, anywhere I go, I have to sing it.
It's as much a part of me as my floppy ears."

When the United States joined World War II, Bing recorded weekly programs specifically for the Armed Forces Radio Service. All the recordings were pressed on extra-large military records called V-Discs and shipped to troops fighting overseas. Bing traveled to Europe to entertain the weary, homesick soldiers. He told jokes and sang for hours at a time. The most requested song was "White Christmas."

"I had to sing 'White Christmas' for 15,000 GIs in tears and not break up myself. It was the hardest thing I've ever had to do."

Out of all the entertainers to visit the front lines, the troops voted Bing as their favorite actor. Hundreds of soldiers and their families wrote Bing letters. He personally replied to each one.

"The audience of soldiers was the greatest I had ever faced. We left there knowing we'd just been given the rare privilege of bringing even a small touch of home, a few laughs, and some sighs to a wonderful bunch of men doing a sensational job."

The US military even broadcasted Bing speaking in German over European radio, urging the German people to stop the war.

After the war, Bing continued his regular radio shows. Each show was performed live, once for East Coast listeners, then repeated three hours later for West Coast listeners. This inefficient time commitment frustrated Bing. He heard about a new machine that created high-quality recordings on magnetic tape reels. He bought the equipment, hired experts, and together they developed the technology to record and edit shows that sounded like live performances without any mistakes.

> "If I made a mistake in singing a song or in the script,
> I could have some fun with it, then retain
> any of the fun that sounded amusing."

On tape, Bing sang happy songs and joked with personal show-business friends like Louis Armstrong and Bob Hope. Up to fifty million listeners tuned in each week to hear Bing playfully tease his guests and poke fun at himself. Bing sometimes transported his studio band from Los Angeles to Spokane to record his radio show while he visited family and friends.

As his popularity grew, Bing worked even when he wasn't singing or acting. He hired experienced people to give him advice about his career and finances. He took their suggestions and followed his own instincts.

"Listen a lot and talk less.
You can't learn anything when you're talking."

Many companies asked Bing to invest in or advertise their products, and soon people wanted to buy whatever Bing suggested: frozen orange juice, ice cream, easy chairs, cars—even ovens!

Bing committed time and money to advance a wide range of sports that he enjoyed, from horse racing to baseball. He became part owner of the World Series-winning Pittsburgh Pirates, sometimes practicing in uniform with the team during spring training. He knew all the players' statistics and minor league prospects.

Bing loved to play his favorite sport, golf, whenever he had the chance. He often rearranged his work schedule and moved filming locations to keep himself near the golf course.

"The only way you can play golf well
is to concentrate completely on what you're doing.
And then you can't really be bothered
by all the other problems of life."

Because Bing was famous, he could play in tournaments with other celebrities and professional golfers. But Bing thought amateurs and professionals should be able to play golf together, so he created and hosted the United States' first national pro and amateur tournament. Average golfers who signed up could play golf with the pros and afterward eat a dinner of baked clams on the beach. Bing called it "Crosby's Clambake," which became the AT&T Pebble Beach Pro-Am, still an annual American tradition.

"Golf brings out the best in a person."

Sadly, Bing's wife, Dixie, died of cancer, and one by one their four sons grew up and left home. A few years later, Bing married a lovely actress named Kathryn Grant. Together, they had two sons and a daughter and moved away from Hollywood. Spending time with his young family delighted Bing.

"The family is the basis for all society. A good family, a good community, and a good nation all work together."

Bing continued making best-selling movies and records. When more Americans began watching television, Bing appeared on several live TV specials. However, he didn't like traveling back and forth to Hollywood for this new job. He asked his magnetic tape-recording experts to help him develop a combination of crisp audio and clear video, advancing technology to an unimagined level. Now, Bing could record a show whenever he wanted, edit out mistakes, add audience responses, and the network could broadcast it later. Bing became the first star to air a television program recorded on videotape.

Charming and comfortable as ever, Bing invited his special Hollywood friends to join him on shows. Bing's friends included Bob Hope, Louis Armstrong, Ella Fitzgerald, Jimmy Stewart, Judy Garland, Peggy Lee, Frank Sinatra, Dean Martin, Sammy Davis Jr., Lucille Ball, and Fred Astaire.

"A friend is one who knows all about you
and loves you just the same."

Bing involved his family in performances, too. His older sons started show business careers, so Bing encouraged them to appear with him. In later years, he, Kathryn, and their three children recorded a musical Christmas special to air each December on national TV.

"There's no feeling warmer, I believe,
than the glow that we get when we open up our hearts
and sing with our families and friends."

For the rest of his life, Bing shared his iconic talent with the world, crooning classic songs and inspiring new ones. Hollywood gave him three stars on the Walk of Fame: one for movies, one for recordings, and one for radio. Bing received many nominations and awards in recognition of his legendary career, including the first-ever Grammy Lifetime Achievement Award.

"I was seeking no great achievement.
I just did what I liked to do."

Despite being the greatest multimedia star of the twentieth century, Bing sang and talked with fans as if they were familiar friends. Bing's smooth, recognizable voice became the most recorded voice in history, reminding listeners of happy times, warm memories, and the classic golden age of entertainment.

"I'm not a legend;
I'm just a fellow who was very lucky
and listened to good advice."

May 3, 1903

Harry Lillis Crosby Jr. is born in Tacoma, Washington, to Harry Lowe Crosby, an accountant, and Catherine Harrigan Crosby. He is the fourth of 7 children.

1906

The Crosby family moves from Tacoma to Spokane, Washington.

1910

Harry earns the nickname "Bingo" (later shortened to "Bing") from a neighbor, Valentine Hobart, inspired by Bing's obsession with a comic strip, *The Bingville Bugle*.

1914

World War I starts.

1917

At age 14, Bing works backstage at Spokane's Auditorium, where he watches performers like Al Jolson, who influences Bing's early style.

1918

World War I ends.

1920

Bing graduates from Gonzaga High School in Spokane and enrolls in pre-law classes at Gonzaga University.

1923

Bing joins the Musicaladers, a local Spokane band, with Al Rinker, performing at Spokane venues, the Clemmer Theater, and on KHQ Radio.

October 1925

Bing and Al Rinker move to Los Angeles to pursue a career in entertainment. Al's sister, famous jazz singer Mildred Bailey, gets auditions for Bing and Al at local night clubs.

1926

Bing and Al join Paul Whiteman's orchestra. Bing records his first single, "I've Got the Girl," with Don Clark's Orchestra (memorable for being recorded at the wrong speed).

1928

Bing and Al join with Harry Barris to form The Rhythm Boys, who continue to perform and record as one of the acts in Paul Whiteman's Orchestra.

1929

The Great Depression begins in the United States.

1930

Bing appears in the early sound film *King of Jazz*.

Bing and The Rhythm Boys separate from Paul Whiteman's Orchestra and begin recording and performing in Los Angeles and New York with popular entertainers like Duke Ellington.

September 29, 1930

Bing marries actress and singer Wilma Winifred Wyatt, known as Dixie Lee, in Los Angeles.

1931

Bing launches his solo radio show *Presenting Bing Crosby* on CBS in New York City, marking the start of his rise to national fame.

Bing records the song, "Out of Nowhere," introducing a new style of singing close to the microphone. The song becomes his first number-one hit.

THE LIFE OF BING CROSBY

1932

Bing stars in *The Big Broadcast*, his first major film role, assisted by his brother Everett's management. His radio performances are broadcast nationally for 20 consecutive weeks.

1933

Bing and Dixie welcome their first son, Gary Evan Crosby.

1934

Twin sons Dennis Michael Crosby and Phillip Lang Crosby are born.

1936

Bing becomes the host of the *Kraft Music Hall* radio program, a role he holds for a decade, solidifying his status as a national star.

Mr. and Mrs. Crosby sell their Spokane home and move to Hollywood, down the street from Bing and his family.

1937

Bing sings "Sweet Leilani," from his hit movie *Waikiki Wedding*, which earns him a gold record, the first of 22 total gold records.

Bing co-founds and becomes part owner of the Del Mar Racetrack in California, greeting fans on opening day at the gate.

Bing's fourth son, Lindsay Harry Crosby, is born.

1938

Julian P. Graham Photo / Pebble Beach Company Lagorio Archives

Bing Crosby sings "Straight Down the Middle" at Pebble Beach

The first Crosby pro-am golf tournament, known as the Crosby Clambake, is held at Rancho Santa Fe, California. Organized by Bing, it combines professional and amateur golfers, including celebrities, with proceeds benefiting charities. The event becomes an annual tradition, moving to Pebble Beach, California, in 1947.

1939

World War II starts.

1940

Bing stars in the comedy film *Road to Singapore*, the first of seven comedy "Road" films with Bob Hope and Dorothy Lamour.

1941

On December 7, Imperial Japan bombs Pearl Harbor, and the United States enters WW II. On Christmas Day, Bing sings "White Christmas" on the radio for the first time publicly.

1942

Bing records "White Christmas" for the film *Holiday Inn*. Released on October 3, 1942, it tops the charts by October 31 and becomes the best-selling single of all time, with estimated sales of over 50 million copies.

1944

Bing stars as Father Charles O'Malley in *Going My Way*, a role that won him an Academy Award for Best Actor in 1945.

Bing Crosby Receives Oscar - 1945

1945

US servicemen polled by *Yank Magazine* vote Bing "the one person who had done the most for wartime morale." The US Army awards Bing the "GI Oscar."

LIFE Magazine names Bing "America's Number One Star" for his unmatched success in music, film, and radio.

World War II ends

1946

Bing purchases a 25% stake in the Pittsburgh Pirates baseball team, becoming a vice president and minority owner for almost 30 years (until his death in 1977).

1947

Bing invests in Ampex, pioneering magnetic tape recording, and begins pre-recording his radio shows, transforming the industry.

Dixie Lee dies of ovarian cancer at age 42.

1948

Bing becomes a major investor in Minute Maid, a company producing frozen orange juice concentrate. He promotes the brand through commercials and a weekday morning radio show called "Minute Maid Fresh Squeezed Orange Juice," which aired from 1949 to 1954.

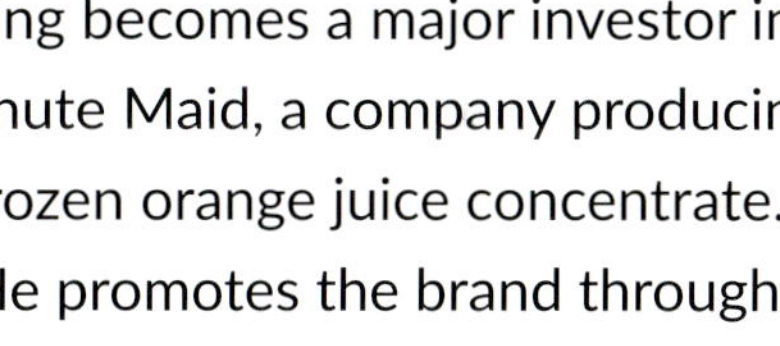

Animated Minute Maid Spot - 1954

1952

Bing Crosby Enterprises Electrical Division invents the first videotape recorder.

Bing receives three stars on the Hollywood Walk of Fame: one for motion pictures, one for radio, and one for recording.

Author Bing publishes his autobiography, *Call Me Lucky*.

1953

Bing records *The Bing Crosby Edsel Show* on videotape and airs it on television. Starring entertainment friends and family to raise funds for the Gonzaga University Library, the show is considered the earliest existing videotape recording.

1957

Bing Crosby films an international TV special, *The Bing Crosby Show*, in London, England, hosting Shirley Bassey and Bob Hope. He performs several popular songs, including "White Christmas." Aired December 11, 1961.

1960

Bing Crosby sings "White Christmas" TV special 1961

1954

Bing stars in *White Christmas* and *The Country Girl*, earning his third and final Academy Award nomination.

October 24, 1957

Bing marries actress Olive Kathryn Grandstaff, known as Kathryn Grant, in Las Vegas.

1958

Bing and Kathryn's first son, Harry Lillis Crosby III, is born.

1959

Bing and Kathryn's first daughter, Mary Frances Crosby, is born.

1961

Bing and Kathryn's son, Nathaniel Patrick Crosby, is born.

1962

Bing becomes the first recipient of the Grammy Lifetime Achievement Award.

1964

Bing hosts *The Hollywood Palace*, a television variety show, and stars in the short-lived sitcom *The Bing Crosby Show* (1964).

1968

Bing is awarded the DeSmet Medal at Gonzaga University and presents the nation's first Microfilm Research Center to the school.

Bing Crosby at Gonzaga 1968

1969

Bing receives a Peabody Award for his contributions to television.

1974

The Bing Crosby on Broadway stage show opens at the Uris Theatre in New York City.

September 1977

Bing films his final Christmas special, *Bing Crosby's Merrie Olde Christmas*, featuring a duet with David Bowie on "Peace on Earth/ Little Drummer Boy." He also records his final album, *Seasons*.

October 14, 1977

After playing 18 holes of golf, Bing dies of a heart attack at age 74 on a golf course near Madrid, Spain.

2024

Posthumously, Bing Crosby's "White Christmas" is re-released as a duet with V, a member of the South Korean boy band BTS. This version blends V's soulful vocals with Crosby's 1950 recording. Applying advanced technology, the single tops Billboard's charts and introduces Crosby's timeless legacy to new generations.

LEARN MORE ABOUT BING CROSBY

Hear Bing's Timeless Hits Scan to listen to a playlist of Bing Crosby's songs or enjoy some of his classic radio shows from the 1950s.

Explore Bing's Official Website Scan to take a closer look at Bing's career, discography, and see how he is still making news today.

FROM THE AUTHOR, LAUREN R. HARRIS

When I was growing up, everyone had to wait until December each year for the TV stations to play Christmas movies, including *White Christmas*. I loved watching Bing Crosby steal the show; his unmistakable voice filled the room with witty dialogue and vintage-sounding songs. Other than his blue eyes and boo-boo-boo-boos, I didn't know much about Bing until I moved to Spokane and discovered that he grew up like a lot of kids, living in an average home while dreaming big dreams. His Academy Award and gold records speak for themselves, but more valuable and lasting are both his humble words about himself and what people remember about his character: Bing was kind, generous, and the same person whether on or off the stage. That's what I truly admire.

FROM THE ILLUSTRATOR, JOE EVERSON

When I was young, I told my art teacher that I didn't have to follow her instruction because "art can be anything." She responded, "The best artists learn the rules, so they know how to break them." Years later, I learned she was quoting Pablo Picasso. Like Picasso, I wanted to learn how to paint every style, every medium, and every subject. I think you'll see that in how I approached the art in this story. What a joy to be a part of this book and show Bing Crosby in a way he's never been seen before. I hope my paintings communicate his fun-loving spirit and capture not only Bing's personality but also inspire young readers to explore his timeless music and films.

ACKNOWLEDGMENTS

SPECIAL THANKS TO Robert Bader, HLC Properties, LTD; Bing Crosby Advocates; Mary Crosby; The Everson Family; Gonzaga University; The Harris Family; International Club Crosby; Daniel Lyles; Melinda Martin; Northside Writer's Group; Pebble Beach Company Archives; The Pickett Fence; Stephanie Plowman; Primary Wave; The Reed Family.

RESOURCES

Resources listed below used for content development, as well as sourcing of quotes throughout the book, as noted below. Some quotes have been modified without changing their meaning.

Crosby, Bing. Interview with Fletcher Markle. *Telescope*. CBC, January 13, 1966.
- "A friend is one who knows . . ."

Crosby, Bing. Interview with Edward R. Murrow. *Person to Person*, CBS, December 3, 1954.
- "When you're doing what you like to do . . ."

Crosby, Bing. Interview with Ed Sullivan. *The Ed Sullivan Show*, CBS, July 15, 1956.
- "Anybody who wants to be a singer . . ."

Crosby, Bing. Interview with Judy Allan. FETV Scotland, June 1976.
- "I'm not a legend . . ."
- "I guess I started singing . . ."
- "The family is the basis . . ."

Crosby, Bing. Interview with Joe Franklin, *The Joe Franklin Show*, WWOR-TV, 1976.
- "The only way you can play golf well . . ."

Crosby, Bing. Letter to Mrs. Philip K. Lawler. February 28, 1941.
- "The audience of soldiers . . ."

Crosby, Bing. "You Could Hurt Bing But He'd Sing Anyhow." *Des Moines Tribune*, August 23, 1934.
- "I love to sing, and I can thank my lucky stars . . ."

Crosby, Bing, and Pete Martin. *Call Me Lucky: Bing Crosby's Own Story*. New York: Simon & Schuster, 1953.
- "Although I wasn't a musician . . ."
- "It's a great song with a simple melody . . ."
- "If I made a mistake in singing a song . . ."
- "I was seeking no great . . ."
- "Golf brings out the best . . ."
- "All a man can do . . ."
- "Every person's life . . ."

Crosby, Howard. Interview with Brie Stimson, Fox News, December 21, 2024.
- "I had to sing 'White Christmas' for 15,000 GIs . . ."

Crosby, Ted. *The Story of Bing Crosby*. Cleveland: The World Publishing Company, 1946.
- "I told my parents I would rather . . ."

Giddins, Gary. *Bing Crosby: A Pocketful of Dreams, The Early Years, 1903–1940*. New York: Back Bay Books, 2001.
- "I had a constant succession . . ."
- "We had a lot of experience . . ."

Grover Bell, Jesse. *Here's How by Who's Who: How to Succeed by 101 Men Who Did*. Madison, WI: University of Wisconsin Madison, 1968.
- "Listen a lot and talk less . . ."

Sullivan, Ed, and Betty Sullivan Precht. *Christmas with Ed Sullivan*. New York: McGraw-Hill Book Company, Inc., 1959.
- "I have traveled many different . . ."

OSBY RANCH
ELKO
EVADA

For The Largest Number Of Their
Favorite Stars Of Any Company—3 Out Of
The Top 5—In Photoplay Magazine's
Annual National Election
This is the authoritative voice of the public thru the most extensive survey of popular taste of any poll. Again this year ticket-buyer preference honors the Star Company and these 3 great Star Favorites.
BING CROSBY
ALAN LADD
BOB HOPE
"A CONNECTICUT YANKEE"
"WHISPERING SMITH"
"SORROWFUL JONES"

"ALL-STAR BOND RALLY"
19 Minutes of Big-Time Entertainment
VIVIAN BLAINE · JEANNE CRAIN
BING CROSBY · LINDA DARNELL
BETTY GRABLE · JUNE HAVER
BOB HOPE · HARRY JAMES
FAYE MARLOW · HARPO MARX
FIBBER McGEE and MOLLY
CARMEN MIRANDA · FRANK SINATRA

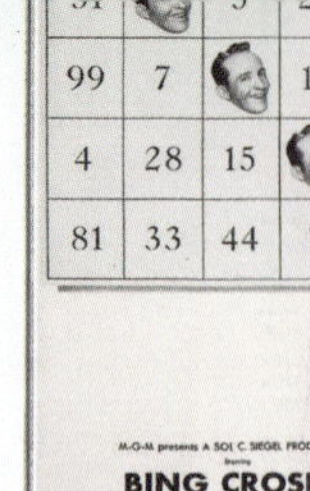
BING CROSB
"MAN ON FIR

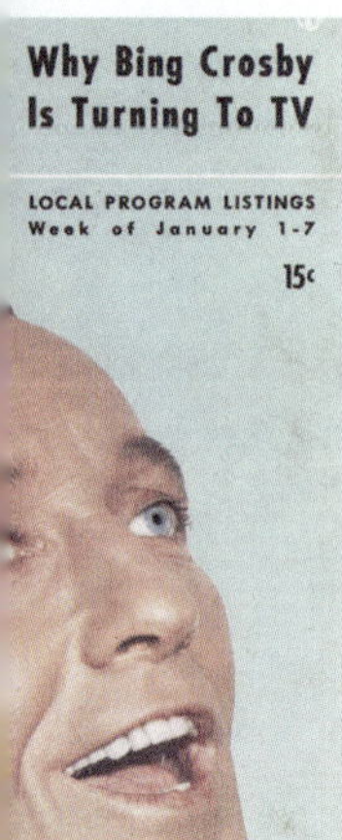
Why Bing Crosby Is Turning To TV
LOCAL PROGRAM LISTINGS
Week of January 1-7
15¢

BING and his PIRATES
BY JACK SHER

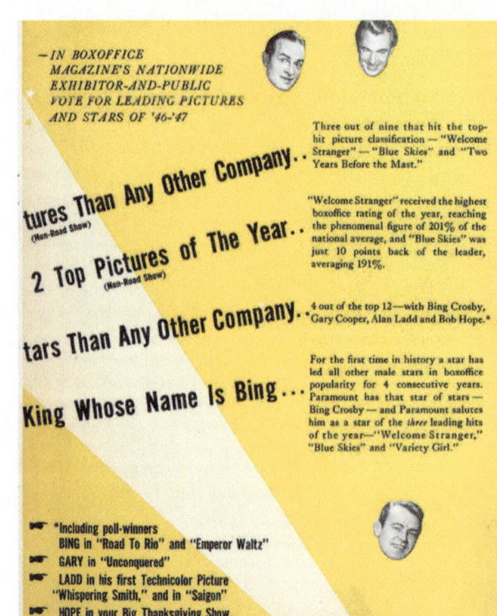
IN BOXOFFICE MAGAZINE'S NATIONWIDE EXHIBITOR-AND-PUBLIC VOTE FOR LEADING PICTURES AND STARS OF '46-'47
tures Than Any Other Company..
2 Top Pictures of The Year..
tars Than Any Other Company..
King Whose Name Is Bing...

Bing Finally Gives In To TV

Spoka

NOT DRESSING"

Announcing THE GOLD
America's Most Popular Stars

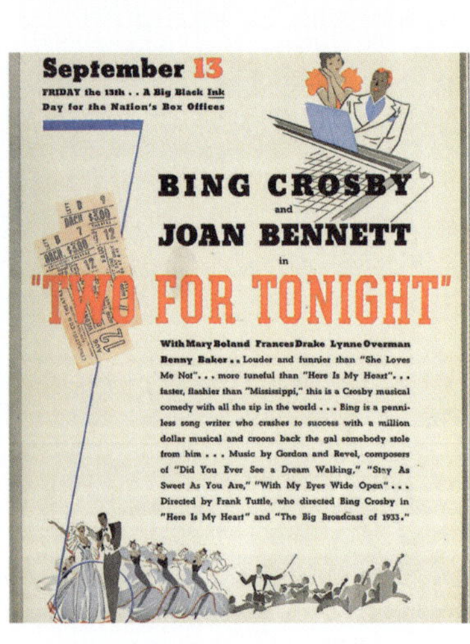
September 13
BING CROSBY
and
JOAN BENNETT
in
"TWO FOR TONIGHT"

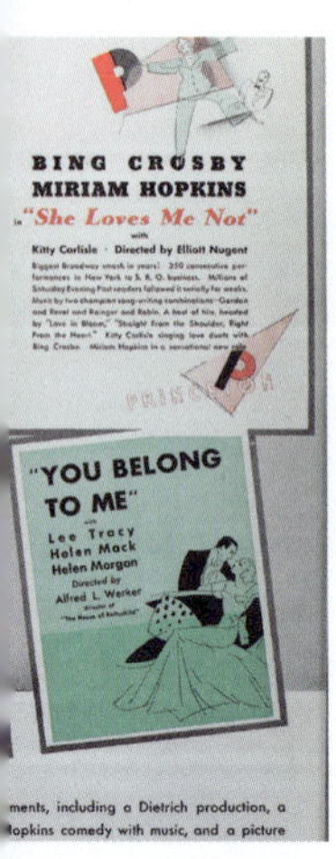
BING CROSBY
MIRIAM HOPKINS
"She Loves Me Not"
"YOU BELONG TO ME"

Crosby Day at Pebble Beach

CROSBY'S VIDEO TAPE RECORDER

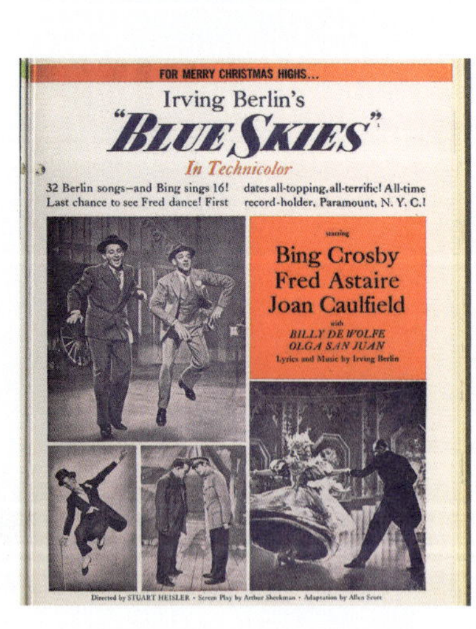
FOR MERRY CHRISTMAS HIGHS...
Irving Berlin's
"BLUE SKIES"
In Technicolor
32 Berlin songs—and Bing sings 16! Last chance to see Fred dance! First
dates all-topping, all-terrific! All-time record-holder, Paramount, N. Y. C.!
Bing Crosby
Fred Astaire
Joan Caulfield

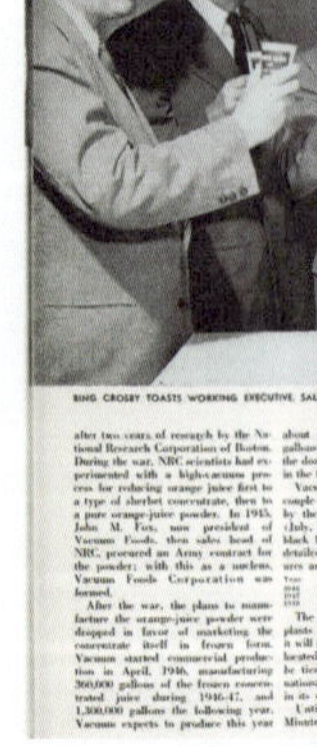

THRILLS

Photo-Plays
A Bing Crosby-Barry Fitzgerald Adventure Told in Comics

FOR 1946

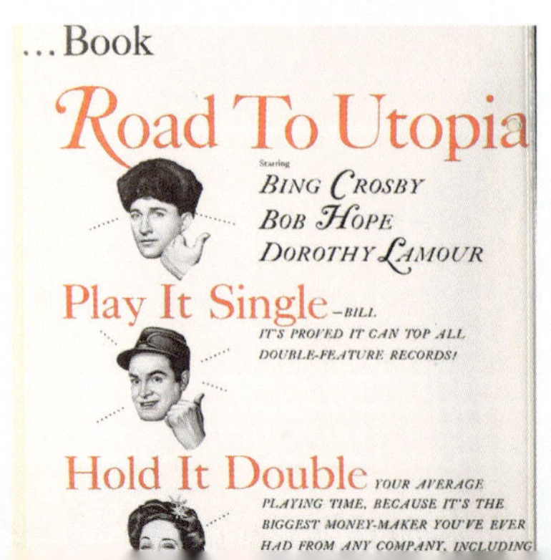
...Book
Road To Utopia
BING CROSBY
BOB HOPE
DOROTHY LAMOUR
Play It Single
Hold It Double